Color Your Way to a Life You Love™

CRUSH SELF-DOUBT

A SELF-HELP ADULT COLORING BOOK FOR RELAXATION & PERSONAL GROWTH!

60 CALMING DESIGNS TO COLOR!
FLOWERS & NATURE
ANIMALS
MANDALAS
DOODLES & PATTERNS

COLOR YOUR WAY TO A LIFE YOU LOVE™: CRUSH SELF-DOUBT

For information:
shellijohnson.com
alphadollmedia.com

Copyright Notice and Disclaimers

This book is Copyright © 2018 Shelli Johnson (the "Author"). All Rights Reserved. Published in the United States of America. The legal notices, disclosures, and disclaimers within this book are copyrighted by the Internet Attorneys Association LLC and licensed for use by the Author in this book. All rights reserved.

No part of this book may be reproduced or transmitted in any form or by any means, electronic or mechanical, including photocopying, recording, or by an information storage and retrieval system — except by a reviewer who may quote brief passages in a review to be printed in a magazine, newspaper, blog, or website — without permission in writing from the Author. For information, please contact the Author at the following website address: shellijohnson.com/contact

For more information, please read the "Disclosures and Disclaimers" section at the end of this book.

First Paperback Print Edition, April 2018

Published by Alpha Doll Media, LLC (the "Publisher").

ISBN: 978-0-9747109-9-0

WELCOME TO THE
COLOR YOUR WAY TO A LIFE YOU LOVE™
COLORING BOOK SERIES!

  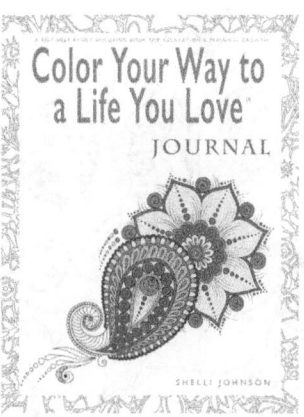

AVAILABLE NOW OR COMING SOON!

UNLEASH YOUR INNER CREATOR & MAKE IT YOUR OWN!

This is not just another coloring book, it's also an invitation for you to delve deeper into who you are so you can find out what makes you come alive. I'm a big believer in the power of taking small steps to get you anywhere you need or want to go. With that in mind, I invite you inside these pages on a creative self-help adventure. You'll unleash your artistic side with designs and patterns while you do daily small-sized activities aimed at: 1. helping you heal yourself and 2. inspiring you to create a life you love. My hope is that you'll use these pages to ignite your imagination, discard your limitations, and free your inner creator.

Feel free to add your own personal embellishments to any image. You can make each page as unique as you like by adding doodles, patterns, and/or shapes. Color the images any way you like with any tools you like. There are no rules except that you relax, enjoy, and color in a way that feels right to you.

THE MEANING & PURPOSE OF LIFE!

"The meaning of life is to find your gift. The purpose of life is to give it away."
—Pablo Picasso

THE PSYCHOLOGY OF COLOR!

From my layman's understanding of the meaning of colors, certain colors can evoke certain emotions.

BLUE: centered, calm, hopeful, confidence
GREEN: growth, safety, endurance, calm
ORANGE: energy, happiness, encouragement, excitement
RED: passion, energy, strength, power, determination
YELLOW: joy, energy, cheerfulness
BROWN: stability
PURPLE: power, ambition, creativity, energy
BLACK: power, elegance, mystery
WHITE: light, goodness, safety

So keep that in mind as you color. If you're looking to experience a particular emotion/feeling/mood, you may want to use a particular color to help you get there.

A FEW HELPFUL SUGGESTIONS!

BABY STEPS
I'm a big believer in the power of taking baby steps to get you anywhere you need or want to go, which is why this coloring book is written the way it is. Each day has small-sized activities. They build on each other, one to the next. So feel free to color whichever image you'd like, just know you'll be best served to do the daily activities in order.

NO PERFECTION NEEDED
Do yourself a kindness and make a mistake in this coloring book early on. Scribble on some of the pages. Spill your favorite beverage on the cover. Rip one of the corners off. Color outside the lines. Make this book imperfect so that you'll feel free to be your real, honest self inside the pages. Being real, not being perfect, is what's going to heal you and set you free.

BE HONEST
I'd recommend that you don't show your answers inside this coloring book to anyone. Keep them to yourself for right now until you make it all the way through Day 30. Why? Honesty with yourself is what's going to help you heal and grow. You won't be completely honest if you're worried about someone reading your answers. In fact, what you're likely to do is tweak your responses, edit them, or scratch them out entirely if you're worried about how others might perceive you. So be kind to yourself & let this coloring book be just for you.

BE WILLING & OPEN
The first step to change is to be open & willing to it. You picked up this coloring book because you're struggling in this area of your life. If you want things to be different, well, both you & those things are going to have to change. So be open to experiencing something new & be willing to do the effort to get there.

GIVE YOURSELF PERMISSION
It's hugely important to give yourself permission (whether that's verbally or written) to: do the daily steps in this book, be/have/do/say/believe whatever you need to so that you can heal yourself, give yourself unlimited tries as many times as it takes, believe in your own worth and value, choose to create a life you love because you matter. Whenever you feel like you need someone else's permission to make a choice about your life, you just give that permission to yourself. The only permission you ever need to live your own life is your own.

YOU'RE ON A JOURNEY
It doesn't matter how old you are, how many times you've tried, or how far there is left to go. It's never too late to be the person you want to be. It's okay if you don't know things yet. You're on a journey and you'll figure it out as you go. This coloring book is designed to help you do just that.

BEGIN YOUR DAY WITH A STEP
If at all possible, do your daily step shortly after you wake up. That way, you'll be able to focus on yourself (because you're absolutely worth the time to do that) before your day gets away from you. So grab your favorite beverage. Find a quiet place. Relax and reflect while you're being creative.

IT'S A PRACTICE & A PROCESS
There's no doing this perfectly, and that's okay. You strive for progress. You do the best you can. So show yourself some patience and kindness because self-compassion is what you most need to heal yourself. You will make mistakes, there's just no way around it. Don't ever use any mistake as a reason to give up on yourself. Just circle back around and start again. And know this: every mistake is simply a brand new chance to do it better the next time.

AND FINALLY . . .
Remember (not just for this book but for all of life): you get out what you put in. So make yourself a priority in your own life because: 1. you're absolutely worth the effort and 2. no one else can do it for you. And one last suggestion good both for this book and for all of life: be brave and color outside the lines, that's where freedom lies.

THOSE WHO ARE BRAVE ARE FREE!

"It is not the critic who counts; not the man who points out how the strong man stumbles, or where the doer of deeds could have done them better. The credit belongs to the man who is actually in the arena, whose face is marred by dust and sweat and blood; who strives valiantly; who errs, who comes short again and again, because there is no effort without error and shortcoming; but who does actually strive to do the deeds; who knows great enthusiasms, the great devotions; who spends himself in a worthy cause; who at the best knows in the end the triumph of high achievement, and who at the worst, if he fails, at least fails while daring greatly, so that his place shall never be with those cold and timid souls who neither know victory nor defeat."
—Theodore Roosevelt

Source: excerpt (also known as *The Man In The Arena*) from the speech "Citizenship in a Republic" delivered at The Sorbonne in Paris, France on April 23, 1910.

COLOR TEST PAGE

Slow and steady wins the race.
—Aesop

It does not matter how slowly you go
as long as you do not stop.
—Confucius

1
1. Today, relax.
2. Take a deep breath in through your nose.
3. Hold it for three seconds.
4. Let it out through your mouth.
5. Then pull your shoulders down away from your ears.
6. Repeat five times.
7. Massage your temples & the back of your neck.
8. Repeat often, especially every time you feel self-doubt rise up in you.

2

1. Today, know that you are not alone.
2. You may feel alone. You may feel like everyone else is boldly & confidently moving forward in their lives while you steep in self-doubt.
3. But know this: you are likely comparing others' outsides to your insides (& comparison is an act of self-abuse). You also don't know just how long they were (& maybe still are) struggling with self-doubt before they broke free.
4. So don't be so hard on yourself. Instead, remind yourself that you're not alone, that you are in fact in excellent company with the rest of us who are/have been hindered or stopped by self-doubt, as often as needed.

3

1. Today, believe in your own worth & value.
2. Know this: your worth & value are innate. You were born with them. You don't have to have/be/do/say any certain thing to earn them & nobody — hear me, *nobody* — can ever take them away from you. Regardless of what happens to you during your lifetime, your worth & value will still, & forever, be intact.
3. Write this: *I always have worth & value. I am enough as-is. I am alive for a reason. I have a purpose. I matter & what I do matters. My worth & value are forever intact.*
4. Then honor & respect yourself by choosing (yes, it's a choice) to repeat those facts over & over until they become the beliefs that guide your life.

4

1. Today, listen for the voice of wisdom inside you.
2. Know this: your voice of wisdom (also known as your intuition) is the one that's kind, nurturing, & supportive. Your voice of wisdom will *never* tear you down or berate you or harm you. It will *never* fuel your self-doubt. *Ever.* Instead, it will *always* strengthen you, encourage you, & help you grow.
3. So take at least 15 minutes to be alone. Listen for your intuition & quickly (so no overthinking or editing) write answers to these: *What do I honestly believe about my chances? My abilities? My gifts & talents? My place in the world?*

*Look in a mirror. Say: *I always have worth & value. I have a purpose. I matter.******

1. Today, pay attention to your internal dialogue.
2. Take at least 15 minutes to be alone & write down any chatter inside your head that's fueling your self-doubt.
3. Know this: you will live out whatever it is you're repeating to yourself. That's true regardless of what others are saying to &/or about you. Tell yourself you can't & you won't. Tell yourself you can, even if you have to say it over & over again, & eventually you will. Tell yourself you don't have what it takes & you'll quit. Tell yourself you're able &, even if it's hard, you'll keep going.

*Look in a mirror. Say: *I always have worth & value. I have a purpose. I matter.**

1. Today, be your own champion & speak strength to yourself.
2. Today & *every day*, be thoughtful & deliberate before you speak about yourself. Now read through your answers from Days 4 & 5.
3. Remember: you *always* get to choose what you allow or don't allow in your mind. So write: *I am*. Then finish that sentence with what you want to think/believe about yourself (like: *capable, strong, intelligent, determined, brave, tenacious, committed,* etcetera). Repeat those new words/phrases to yourself.
4. Know this: you will be victorious or defeated by what you tell yourself.

*Look in a mirror. Say: *I always have worth & value. I have a purpose. I matter.**

7

1. Today, build a support system.
2. Write a list of people *whom you trust* to strengthen & encourage you.
3. Reach out to at least one person on that list today. Tell them that you struggle with self-doubt. Ask if you can contact them whenever you need a pep talk.
4. Or you can join/start a support group (even if it's just you & one other person) that meets regularly for encouragement. Also, you can *always* choose to befriend yourself, encouraging & strengthening yourself by telling yourself, in any given moment, words that you most need to hear.

Believe in your worth & value. Speak strength to yourself.

8

1. Today, keep your word & your commitments.
2. Answer this: *Would I put my life in the hands of someone I didn't trust?*
3. Know this: your life is already in your hands; it's up to you how you want to live it. The quickest way to earn your own trust is to keep your word & your commitments to yourself. Say you're going to do something then do it. Say you believe something then stand your ground & defend it.
4. So write this: *I resolve today & every day to keep my word & my commitments to myself every single time.* Then take action & do just that from now on.

Believe in your worth & value. Speak strength to yourself.

9

1. Today, choose faith not fear (because faith is the opposite of fear).
2. Know this: self-doubt is just fear dressed up as something else. Fear says: you can't, you don't have what it takes. Fear asks in a snarky tone: *Just who do I think I am?* Faith is believing you can & you should. It's believing that you have worth & value, that you are alive for a reason & have a purpose, that you matter & what you do matters. Faith asks in a quiet voice: *Who am I not to be?*
3. Write this: *I commit today & every day to choose self-faith over self-doubt.* Then take action & do just that from now on.

Believe in your worth & value. Speak strength to yourself.

10

1. Today, trust yourself.
2. Know this: self-doubt is often used as a way to stay inside your comfort zone. But there are no guarantees of either comfort or safety in nature. Life will still befall you while you're in your comfort zone. The only way to crush self-doubt is to move & keep moving, slow & steady, through it.
3. So *always* be willing to step outside of your comfort zone & into the unknown. Believe today & *every day* that you're capable, trustworthy, & strong enough to take care of yourself & handle whatever life brings your way (because you are).

Believe in your worth & value. Speak strength to yourself.

11

1. Today, decide what matters deeply to you.
2. Write down a list of your deepest hopes/dreams/goals/desires/ideas/etcetera. Include your own unique gifts & talents, things you are passionate about, things you love to do or that light a spark in you, those times in your life when you're happiest & feel the most alive.
3. Then, with that list at the top of your mind, write an answer to this: *If I wasn't full of self-doubt, what would I be doing with my life?*
4. Write down what you would like to have/be/do/say. Be specific.

Believe in your worth & value. Speak strength to yourself.

12

1. Today, approve of your own hopes/dreams/goals/desires/ideas/etcetera.
2. Know this: seeking out others to approve of your plans &/or give you permission is a procrastination tactic that only fuels self-doubt.
3. Read through your list from Day 11. Put a star next to each one that you're putting off, waiting for others to reassure you that it's worthwhile.
4. The only permission you ever need to have/be/do/say what deeply matters to you is your own, because wanting something for your life is reason enough.
5. Make your own happiness & well-being your motivation as you move forward.

Believe in your worth & value. Speak strength to yourself.

13

1. Today, define the direction in which you want to go.
2. Read through your list from Day 11. Now circle *one* item that deeply matters to you that you're the most passionate about working on & *finishing*.
3. Envision the best possible outcome of that hope/dream/goal/desire/idea/etcetera. Starting from that endpoint, work your way backward to today & write down all the steps you can think of that will get you from where you are now to where you envision that best possible outcome to be. If you feel self-doubt or fear, the step you're making is too big. So just make it smaller.

Believe in your worth & value. Speak strength to yourself.

14

1. Today, take action & move through self-doubt.
2. Read through your list of steps from Day 13. Take a deep breath in through your nose, hold it for three seconds, then let it out your mouth.
3. Take the first step today. From now on, take another step (the next one on the list) *every single day* — one small step after another — *until you finish*.
4. Always aim for progress, not perfection. It truly doesn't matter how slowly you go as long as you move forward & you don't stop until you've finished.
5. Remember: move & keep moving, slow & steady, & you'll crush self-doubt.

Believe in your worth & value. Speak strength to yourself.

15

1. Today, play to your strengths.
2. Know this: we all have weaknesses, things we're just not good at. Self-doubt often happens when you focus on your weaknesses instead of your strengths.
3. Make two columns: STRENGTHS on one side, WEAKNESSES on the other.
4. Read your list from Day 13. With that list in mind, write down your strengths & your weaknesses to achieving those things that matter deeply to you.
5. From this point forward, focus on & take action with your strengths. Do yourself a kindness: ask others for help & delegate your weaknesses.

Believe in your worth & value. Speak strength. Take action, slow & steady.

16

1. Today, acknowledge that your life is finite.
2. Know this: your life belongs to you & you alone. Someday it will be over. There's just not that kind of time to keep putting things off.
3. Know this too: procrastination is just fear that stops forward progress. Self-doubt is often used as an excuse to procrastinate. Procrastination then fuels even more self-doubt. Remember: *to crush self-doubt, you must move through it.*
4. Now contact someone from the support system you built on Day 7 & ask for what you need (like encouragement/expertise/funding/laughter/etcetera).

Believe in your worth & value. Speak strength. Take action, slow & steady.

17

1. Today, ban the vampires from your life.
2. Know this: a vampire is a person/place/thing that sucks the life out of you, drains your energy, &/or fuels your self-doubt.
3. Write a list of vampires in your life. You'll know them by the negative way your body reacts &/or the negative way you feel when you're around them.
4. Do yourself a kindness & limit your time with vampires or cut them out of your life entirely. (Yes, you can & need to give yourself permission to do this). Always remember: it's your own life that you're working to save.

Believe in your worth & value. Speak strength. Take action, slow & steady.

18

1. Today, acknowledge your accomplishments.
2. Write a list of any & all achievements/successes/awards/goals met/etcetera (no matter how big or small).
3. Read over that list & let it strengthen & encourage you.
4. Tack that list up where you will see it.
5. Revisit that list every time self-doubt rises up in you.
6. Now go do something nice for you & celebrate all your efforts. Repeat often.

Believe in your worth & value. Speak strength. Take action, slow & steady.

19

1. Today, acknowledge encouraging things others have said about you.
2. Write a list of any & all kind words others have said about you &/or your work. Choose to believe those words.
3. Read over that list & let it strengthen & encourage you.
4. Tack that list up where you will see it.
5. Revisit that list every time self-doubt rises up in you.
6. Now go do something fun that *you* would like to do. Have a great time! Let your mind relax so you can rejuvenate & refresh. Repeat often.

Believe in your worth & value. Speak strength. Take action, slow & steady.

20

1. Today, take the pressure off yourself.
2. Let yourself be a beginner (even if you've been doing something a while) so you can look at your life with fresh eyes &/or from a different perspective. Be open to not knowing everything right now. Be willing to make mistakes & learn as you go. Let experience teach you everything you need to know.
3. Be kind, gentle, & patient with yourself along the way. Don't beat yourself up or lose faith in yourself or fuel your self-doubt. Simply learn & carry on.
4. Make this your mantra from now on: *I believe there is only success or learning.*

Believe in your worth & value. Speak strength. Take action, slow & steady.

21

1. Today, know that your failures don't define you.
2. So write a list of past failures/disappointments/mistakes/criticisms received/unreached goals/etcetera that are fueling your self-doubt.
3. Go down that list & write what you can learn from each one.
4. Now you're better prepared to begin again from a more informed & intelligent perspective. So just pick yourself up, dust yourself off, use what you've learned, & keep moving forward in the direction that you want to go.
5. Befriend yourself & write down five things you *really* need to hear right now.

Believe in your worth & value. Speak strength. Take action, slow & steady.

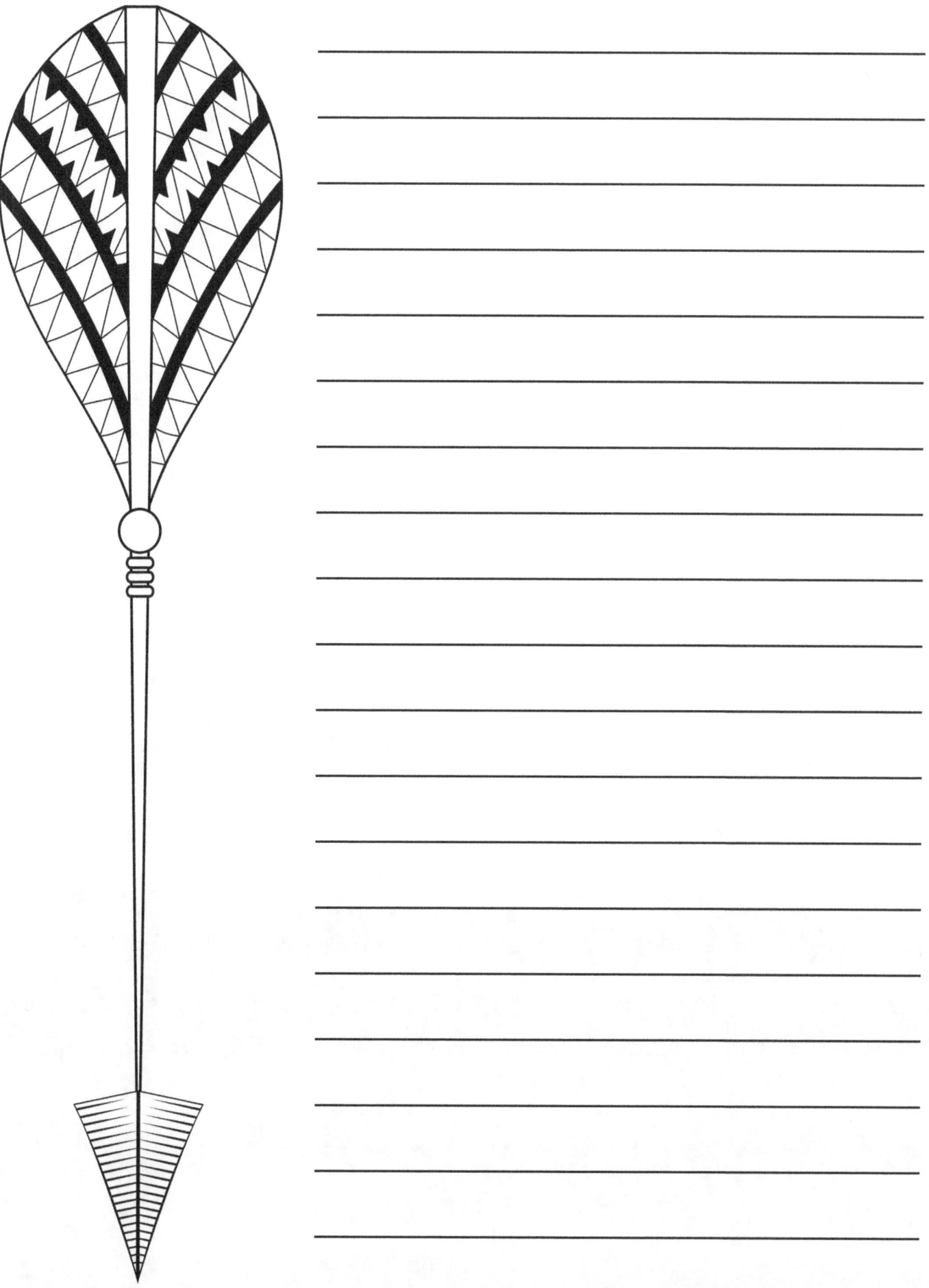

22

1. Today, live in the present moment.
2. Write a list of the parts of your history that you may be hanging on to, especially anything that may be fueling your self-doubt.
3. Write a list of your concerns/fears/worries/etcetera for the future, especially anything that may be fueling your self-doubt.
4. Now, breathe deep & let all that go. The past will teach you so learn from it. The future will give you goals if you let it. The only place you can take any action to make forward progress & move through self-doubt is right now.

Believe in your worth & value. Speak strength. Take action, slow & steady.

23

1. Today, believe your opinion of yourself is the only one that matters.
2. Know this: you'll never truly be free until you stop being concerned about what others think of you &/or until you stop trying to impress others.
3. Write a list of areas where you're concerned about what others think of you &/or you're striving to impress others. Now write how you've tweaked your actions/beliefs/goals/personality/etcetera to better suit the opinions of others.
4. Choose to honor & respect yourself by no longer being enslaved to the opinions of others. Choose to free yourself so you can be yourself.

Believe in your worth & value. Speak strength. Take action, slow & steady.

24

1. Today, practice self-kindness & stop comparing yourself with others.
2. Know this: comparison fuels self-doubt & is an act of self-abuse.
3. Write a list of any comparisons you're making. Be honest.
4. Read through that list & take note of how your body feels (small? powerless? defeated? less than?). Take note of your level of self-doubt too.
5. Now read through your lists from Days 18 & 19. Focus on & repeat to yourself all those things that are awesome about you.
6. If you find yourself comparing again, *gently* remind yourself to stop.

Believe in your worth & value. Speak strength. Take action, slow & steady.

25

1. Today, aim for progress not perfection.
2. Know this: perfectionism is just fear about proving your self-worth. Remember: your worth & value are innate. You do not have to prove your worth to anyone, *ever*. Perfectionism does not increase your worth & value one bit. All perfectionism does is fuel self-doubt & delay.
3. Write a list of areas in your life where you're stuck waiting for things to be perfect. Next to each, write your fears about moving forward imperfectly in those areas. For each fear, write a supportive response like a friend would say.

Believe in your worth & value. Speak strength. Take action, slow & steady.

26

1. Today, surrender the outcome.
2. Know this: you have no control over what others will think/do/say. All you can control is this: your own actions, striving for your own progress, & doing your best with every endeavor.
3. Write a list of the outcomes you're hoping for, struggling against, &/or trying to control. Know that you're putting your power in the hands of others.
4. Take your power back by letting go of specific outcomes. Take the pressure off yourself so you can relax into your life & find joy again.

Believe in your worth & value. Speak strength. Take action, slow & steady.

27

1. Today, look in the direction that you're headed.
2. So look forward.
3. Read through your list from Day 11.
4. On a new page, reorder that list from most important to you to least important to you. Tack that list up where you'll see & read through it *daily*.
5. That list is where you are headed. That is forward for you.
6. Remember: you're headed that way for *yourself* because those things matter deeply to *you* & that's reason enough.

Believe in your worth & value. Speak strength. Take action, slow & steady.

28

1. Today, empower yourself by being persistent.
2. Know this: persistence is the only way you'll ever discover just what you're capable of & how much potential you really have. You will crush self-doubt & prove to yourself just how much you believe in yourself if you'll simply persist & carry on, if you'll simply keep going until you finish.
3. So read your list from Day 15 & *always* play to your strengths. Then keep moving & taking action, slow & steady, for every item on your Day 27 list.
4. Now have your own back *always* & refuse to give up on yourself *ever*.

Believe in your worth & value. Speak strength. Take action, slow & steady.

29

1. Today, choose to be brave.
2. Know this: the critics are *not* the ones who count. You, who is doing the work & putting it out into the world, are the one who deserves the credit (see the *Those Who Are Brave Are Free* quote near the beginning of this book).
3. Do what you love — work that *deeply matters to you*, because that is reason enough — to the absolute best of your ability. Breathe deep, have courage, & share your work (finished or not) with someone on your list from Day 7.
4. Keep going, slow & steady, until you finish. Share your work with the world.

Believe in your worth & value. Speak strength. Take action, slow & steady.

30

1. Today, celebrate!
2. Be proud of yourself for how far you've come.
3. Write down your successes & victories (big or small).
4. Do something nice for yourself (like a prize for a job well done).
5. Go & enjoy your life!

Believe in your worth & value. Speak strength. Take action, slow & steady.

ABOUT THE AUTHOR!

This book was born out of Shelli Johnson's own struggle with self-doubt. She wanted and needed to heal herself. She wanted and needed practical and easy steps she could take to believe in herself again so she could conquer her insecurities and forge ahead with confidence. So she simply wrote the book she needed to read. Every day, she does her best to cut herself some slack & practice progress, not perfection.

Shelli's also an award-winning journalist (sports reporting), novelist (grand prize winner), and blogger (shellijohnson.com/blog). She's a truck owner, horse rider, photographer, yoga enthusiast, and slow-cooker fan (shellijohnson.com/recipes). Find out more at: shellijohnson.com/about

Find out about Shelli's other books at:
shellijohnson.com/books

GET YOUR FREE STUFF!

Visit: shellijohnson.com/signup
Opt-in for the newsletter to keep in touch.
Get a free bookmark to color.

ACKNOWLEDGMENTS!

My sincere thanks to people who make my days brighter:
Rollin Johnson
Heather Porazzo

Disclosures and Disclaimers

This book is published in print format. All trademarks and service marks are the properties of their respective owners. All references to these properties are made solely for editorial purposes. Except for marks actually owned by the Author or the Publisher, no commercial claims are made to their use, and neither the Author nor the Publisher is affiliated with such marks in any way.

Unless otherwise expressly noted, none of the individuals or business entities mentioned herein has endorsed the contents of this book.

Limits of Liability & Disclaimers of Warranties

Because this book is a general educational information product, it is not a substitute for professional advice on the topics discussed in it.

The materials in this book are provided "as is" and without warranties of any kind either express or implied. The Author and the Publisher disclaim all warranties, express or implied, including, but not limited to, implied warranties of merchantability and fitness for a particular purpose. The Author and the Publisher do not warrant that defects will be corrected. The Author does not warrant or make any representations regarding the use or the results of the use of the materials in this book in terms of their correctness, accuracy, reliability, or otherwise. Applicable law may not allow the exclusion of implied warranties, so the above exclusion may not apply to you.

Under no circumstances, including, but not limited to, negligence, shall the Author or the Publisher be liable for any special or consequential damages that result from the use of, or the inability to use this book, even if the Author, the Publisher, or an authorized representative has been advised of the possibility of such damages. Applicable law may not allow the limitation or exclusion of liability or incidental or consequential damages, so the above limitation or exclusion may not apply to you. In no event shall the Author or Publisher total liability to you for all damages, losses, and causes of action (whether in contract, tort, including but not limited to, negligence or otherwise) exceed the amount paid by you, if any, for this book.

You agree to hold the Author and the Publisher of this book, principals, agents, affiliates, and employees harmless from any and all liability for all claims for damages due to injuries, including attorney fees and costs, incurred by you or caused to third parties by you, arising out of the products, services, and activities discussed in this book, excepting only claims for gross negligence or intentional tort.

You agree that any and all claims for gross negligence or intentional tort shall be settled solely by confidential binding arbitration per the American Arbitration Association's commercial arbitration rules. Your claim cannot be aggregated with third party claims. All arbitration must occur in the municipality where the Author's principal place of business is located. Arbitration fees and costs shall be split equally, and you are solely responsible for your own lawyer fees.

Facts and information are believed to be accurate at the time they were placed in this book. All data provided in this book is to be used for information purposes only. The information contained within is not intended to provide specific legal, financial, tax, physical or mental health advice, or any other advice whatsoever, for any individual or company and should not be relied upon in that regard. The services described are only offered in jurisdictions where they may be legally offered. Information provided is not all-inclusive, and is limited to information that is made available and such information should not be relied upon as all-inclusive or accurate.

For more information about this policy, please contact the Author at the website address listed in the Copyright Notice at the front of this book.

IF YOU DO NOT AGREE WITH THESE TERMS AND EXPRESS CONDITIONS, DO NOT READ THIS BOOK. YOUR USE OF THIS BOOK, INCLUDING PRODUCTS, SERVICES, AND ANY PARTICIPATION IN ACTIVITIES MENTIONED IN THIS BOOK, MEAN THAT YOU ARE AGREEING TO BE LEGALLY BOUND BY THESE TERMS.

Affiliate Compensation & Material Connections Disclosure

This book may contain references to websites and information created and maintained by other individuals and organizations. The Author and the Publisher do not control or guarantee the accuracy, completeness, relevance, or timeliness of any information or privacy policies posted on these websites.

You should assume that all references to products and services in this book are made because material connections exist between the Author or Publisher and the providers of the mentioned products and services ("Provider"). You should also assume that all website links within this book are affiliate links for (a) the Author, (b) the Publisher, or (c) someone else who is an affiliate for the mentioned products and services (individually and collectively, the "Affiliate").

The Affiliate recommends products and services in this book based in part on a good faith belief that the purchase of such products or services will help readers in general.

The Affiliate has this good faith belief because (a) the Affiliate has tried the product or service mentioned prior to recommending it or (b) the Affiliate has researched the reputation of the Provider and has made the decision to recommend the Provider's products or services based on the Provider's history of providing these or other products or services.

The representations made by the Affiliate about products and services reflect the Affiliate's honest opinion based upon the facts known to the Affiliate at the time this book was published.

Because there is a material connection between the Affiliate and Providers of products or services mentioned in this book, you should always assume that the Affiliate may be biased because of the Affiliate's relationship with a Provider and/or because the Affiliate has received or will receive something of value from a Provider.

Perform your own due diligence before purchasing a product or service mentioned in this book.

The type of compensation received by the Affiliate may vary. In some instances, the Affiliate may receive complimentary products (such as a review copy), services, or money from a Provider prior to mentioning the Provider's products or services in this book.

In addition, the Affiliate may receive a monetary commission or non-monetary compensation when you take action by using a website link within in this book. This includes, but is not limited to, when you purchase a product or service from a Provider after going to a website link contained in this book.

Health Disclaimers

As an express condition to reading to this book, you understand and agree to the following terms.

This book is a general educational health-related information product. This book does not contain medical advice.

The book's content is not a substitute for direct, personal, professional medical care and diagnosis. None of the exercises or treatments (including products and services) mentioned in this book should be performed or otherwise used without prior approval from your physician or other qualified professional health care provider.

There may be risks associated with participating in activities or using products and services mentioned in this book for people in poor health or with pre-existing physical or mental health conditions.

Because these risks exist, you will not use such products or participate in such activities if you are in poor health or have a pre-existing mental or physical condition. If you choose to participate in these risks, you do so of your own free will and accord, knowingly and voluntarily assuming all risks associated with such activities.

Earnings & Income Disclaimers
No Earnings Projections, Promises or Representations

For purposes of these disclaimers, the term "Author" refers individually and collectively to the author of this book and to the affiliate (if any) whose affiliate hyperlinks are referenced in this book.

You recognize and agree that the Author and the Publisher have made no implications, warranties, promises, suggestions, projections, representations or guarantees whatsoever to you about future prospects or earnings, or that you will earn any money, with respect to your purchase of this book, and that the Author and the Publisher have not authorized any such projection, promise, or representation by others.

Any earnings or income statements, or any earnings or income examples, are only estimates of what you might earn. There is no assurance you will do as well as stated in any examples. If you rely upon any figures provided, you must accept the entire risk of not doing as well as the information provided. This applies whether the earnings or income examples are monetary in nature or pertain to advertising credits which may be earned (whether such credits are convertible to cash or not).

There is no assurance that any prior successes or past results as to earnings or income (whether monetary or advertising credits, whether convertible to cash or not) will apply, nor can any prior successes be used, as an indication of your future success or results from any of the information, content, or strategies. Any and all claims or representations as to income or earnings (whether monetary or advertising credits, whether convertible to cash or not) are not to be considered as "average earnings".

Testimonials & Examples
Testimonials and examples in this book are exceptional results, do not reflect the typical purchaser's experience, do not apply to the average person and are not intended to represent or guarantee that anyone will achieve the same or similar results. Where specific income or earnings (whether monetary or advertising credits, whether convertible to cash or not), figures are used and attributed to a specific individual or business, that individual or business has earned that amount. There is no assurance that you will do as well using the same information or strategies. If you rely on the specific income or earnings figures used, you must accept all the risk of not doing as well. The described experiences are atypical. Your financial results are likely to differ from those described in the testimonials.

The Economy
The economy, where you do business, on a national and even worldwide scale, creates additional uncertainty and economic risk. An economic recession or depression might negatively affect your results.

Your Success or Lack of It
Your success in using the information or strategies provided in this book depends on a variety of factors. The Author and the Publisher have no way of knowing how well you will do because they do not know you, your background, your work ethic, your dedication, your motivation, your desire, or your business skills or practices. Therefore, neither the Author nor the Publisher guarantees or implies that you will get rich, that you will do as well, or that you will have any earnings (whether monetary or advertising credits, whether convertible to cash or not), at all.

Businesses and earnings derived therefrom involve unknown risks and are not suitable for everyone. You may not rely on any information presented in this book or otherwise provided by the Author or the Publisher, unless you do so with the knowledge and understanding that you can experience significant losses (including, but not limited to, the loss of any monies paid to purchase this book and/or any monies spent setting up, operating, and/or marketing your business activities, and further, that you may have no earnings at all (whether monetary or advertising credits, whether convertible to cash or not).

Forward-Looking Statements
Materials in this book may contain information that includes or is based upon forward-looking statements within the meaning of the Securities Litigation Reform Act of 1995. Forward-looking statements give the Author's expectations or forecasts of future events. You can identify these statements by the fact that they do not relate strictly to historical or current facts. They use words such as "anticipate," "estimate," "expect," "project," "intend," "plan," "believe," and other words and terms of similar meaning in connection with a description of potential earnings or financial performance.

Any and all forward looking statements here or on any materials in this book are intended to express an opinion of earnings potential. Many factors will be important in determining your actual results and no guarantees are made that you will achieve results similar to the Author or anybody else. In fact, no guarantees are made that you will achieve any results from applying the Author's ideas, strategies, and tactics found in this book.

Purchase Price
Although the Publisher believes the price is fair for the value that you receive, you understand and agree that the purchase price for this book has been arbitrarily set by the Publisher or the vendor who sold you this book. This price bears no relationship to objective standards.

Due Diligence
You are advised to do your own due diligence when it comes to making any decisions. Use caution and seek the advice of qualified professionals before acting upon the contents of this book or any other information. You shall not consider any examples, documents, or other content in this book or otherwise provided by the Author or Publisher to be the equivalent of professional advice.

The Author and the Publisher assume no responsibility for any losses or damages resulting from your use of any link, information, or opportunity contained in this book or within any other information disclosed by the Author or the Publisher in any form whatsoever.

YOU SHOULD ALWAYS CONDUCT YOUR OWN INVESTIGATION (PERFORM DUE DILIGENCE) BEFORE BUYING PRODUCTS OR SERVICES FROM ANYONE. THIS INCLUDES PRODUCTS AND SERVICES SOLD VIA WEBSITE LINKS REFERENCED IN THIS BOOK.